All you need to know about Belgium

Copyright © 2024 Jonas Hoffmann-Schmidt. Translation: Linda Amber Chambers.

All rights reserved. This book, including all its parts, is protected by copyright. Any use outside the narrow limits of copyright law is prohibited without the written consent of the author. This book has been created using artificial intelligence to provide unique and informative content.

Disclaimer: This book is for entertainment purposes only. The information, facts and views contained therein have been researched and compiled to the best of our knowledge and belief. Nevertheless, the author and the publisher assume no liability for the accuracy or completeness of the information. Readers should consult with professionals before making any decisions based on this information. Use of this book is the responsibility of the reader.

Introduction 6

The Geographie Belgians 8

The history of Belgium: from its origins to the present day 10

Roman times and Belgica 12

The Franks and the birth of Belgium 14

The Burgundian Rule and the Burgundian Netherlands 16

The Habsburgs and the Spanish Rule 18

The Belgian Revolution of 1830 20

The Emergence of Modern Belgium 23

Belgium in the First World War 26

Belgium in World War II 28

The European Union and Belgium 30

Belgian kings and the monarchy 32

The Belgian Constitution and Politics 34

The education system in Belgium 36

Economy and trade in Belgium 38

Belgian architecture and art 40

The rich tradition of Belgian comics 42

The role of Belgium in world literature 44

The Belgian music scene 46

Religion and Spirituality in Belgium 49

Brussels: The capital of Europe 51

Antwerp: The diamond city 53

Ghent: The charming city of art 55

Bruges: The "Venice of the North" 57

Liège: an industrial city with a history 59

The Ardennes: Belgium's natural paradise 61

The flora and fauna of Belgium 63

Belgian beers: a world of their own 66

Belgian chocolate: the sweet temptation 68

Belgian waffles: a culinary delight 71

Belgian cheese: from mild to spicy 73

The Belgian language: Dutch, French and German 75

The cultural diversity of Belgium 77

Belgian festivals and customs 79

The Belgian fashion industry 81

Arts and crafts in Belgium 84

Belgian folklore and folk music 86

The Belgian Film Industry 88

Sports and leisure in Belgium 90

Belgian hospitality and etiquette 92

Belgian souvenirs and souvenirs 94

The best tourist attractions in Belgium 97

Secret Treasures: Hidden Gems in Belgium 100

Closing remarks 103

Introduction

A country of cultural diversity and historical significance, Belgium is located in the heart of Europe and fascinates with its rich history, diverse cultures and breathtaking landscapes. This book will take you on a fascinating journey through Belgium to teach you everything you need to know about this remarkable country.

Located between Germany, the Netherlands, France and Luxembourg, Belgium occupies a unique position in Europe. It is not only an important political and economic player, but also a country that stands out for its diversity. Belgium is divided into several regions, including Flanders in the north, Wallonia in the south, and the capital region of Brussels, which is a mixture of both cultures. Belgium's linguistic diversity is a notable feature, as Dutch, French, and German are the official languages.

Belgium's history goes back a long way, spanning eras ranging from Roman settlement, through the rule of the Burgundians and Habsburgs, to the declaration of independence in 1830. Belgium has experienced an eventful past, marked by political upheavals, armed conflicts and territorial changes.

Over the years, Belgium has become a major player in European politics and is the seat of the European Union and NATO. This political importance is reflected in the capital Brussels, which functions as the political and economic center of Europe.

But Belgium is much more than just politics and history. The country is known for its culinary delights, including the world-famous Belgian chocolate, the diverse range of beers and the delicious Belgian waffles. Belgian cuisine combines influences from neighbouring countries and offers a wide range of culinary experiences.

The natural beauty of Belgium stretches from the flat plains of Flanders to the hilly Ardennes in the south of the country. Here you will find abundant wildlife and a variety of outdoor activities ranging from hiking and cycling to water sports.

In this book, we will explore all aspects of Belgium, from its history to culture to nature and culinary highlights. We will visit the most important cities, admire the famous sights and immerse ourselves in the local culture. Join us on this journey of discovery through Belgium and get to know a country that has so much more to offer than meets the eye. Welcome to Belgium!

The Geographie Belgians

Belgium, a small country in the heart of Europe, is characterized by a diverse and varied geography. It covers an area of about 30,528 square kilometers and borders a total of four countries: Germany in the east, the Netherlands in the north, Luxembourg in the southeast and France in the southwest. Belgium's location in the middle of these neighbouring countries has had a significant impact on its geography.

The coast of Belgium stretches for about 67 kilometers along the North Sea and forms the northernmost part of the country. Here we find wide sandy beaches, dunes and picturesque seaside resorts such as Ostend and Knokke-Heist. The Belgian coast is a popular destination for tourists who crave relaxation and sea breezes.

In contrast, the flat and largely flat part of Belgium called Flanders stretches from the coast to the interior. This area is characterized by fertile plains and wide fields that are ideal for agriculture. A variety of agricultural products are grown here, including vegetables, fruits, and grains.

In the south of Belgium rise the Ardennes, a low mountain range that covers a large part of the country. This region is characterized by its hilly topography, dense forests, and picturesque river valleys. The Ardennes is a paradise for nature lovers and offers numerous hiking and outdoor activities. The highest point in Belgium, the Signal de Botrange, is also located in the Ardennes and reaches an altitude of 694 meters above sea level.

Belgium has numerous rivers, including the Meuse in the east, the Scheldt in the north and the Escaut in the south. These rivers play an important role in the country's water supply and trade. In addition, there are numerous channels that connect the different regions of Belgium and facilitate the transport of goods.

The climate in Belgium is characterized by maritime influences due to its location on the North Sea. Summers tend to be mild and winters tend to be cool, with temperatures on the coast tending to be more moderate than inland. Rain is frequent throughout the year, resulting in a green and fertile landscape.

In summary, Belgium's geography is impressively diverse, from the flat plains of Flanders to the hilly Ardennes in the south. This diverse topography, combined with its strategic location in Europe, has shaped the country and made it an interesting and attractive travel destination.

The history of Belgium: from its origins to the present day

The history of Belgium is marked by a remarkable diversity and depth that goes back to the country's distant origins. Belgium, as a political entity, has only existed since independence from the Netherlands in 1830, but the region now known as Belgium is a place where numerous cultures, peoples and powers have intersected over the centuries.

Belgium's roots can be traced back to Roman times, when the region was conquered by the Romans as part of the province of Gallia Belgica. This area, inhabited by various Germanic tribes, was given the name Belgica, which later formed the basis for the country's current name.

After the fall of the Roman Empire in the 5th century, the region experienced a period of uncertainty and changing rule. Various Germanic tribes, including the Franks, settled in the area and formed the basis for the future Belgian identity. Christianization under the leadership of missionaries such as St. Amandus contributed to the spread of Christianity.

In the Middle Ages, the region that now includes Belgium became an important scene in European history. It was ruled by various ruling houses, including the Burgundians and the Habsburgs, who integrated the area into their empires. Under the reign of Charles V, the region became part of the Spanish Empire, which led to political and religious tensions.

The period of Spanish rule finally ended in the 17th century, when the region became involved in the Eighty Years' War. In 1830, Belgium declared its independence from the Netherlands and became a sovereign state. Leopold I became the first king of Belgium, and the country experienced a period of reconstruction and political consolidation.

Throughout the 19th and 20th centuries, Belgium played a significant role in European affairs and became a major player in the Industrial Revolution. During the First World War, Belgium was the scene of devastating battles and later became the seat of important international institutions such as the European Union and NATO.

The history of Belgium is marked by political upheaval, cultural diversity and a unique geographical location in Europe. Today, Belgium is a country that is proud of its history and its role in the European community. It is a place where the past is present in the present in many ways and continues to influence the country's rich culture.

Roman times and Belgica

The Roman era in the region now known as Belgium was of great importance in the historical development of this country. The Romans entered the area they called Gallia Belgica in the 1st century BC, leaving behind a deep cultural and structural influence that shaped the region for centuries.

During Roman rule, Gallia Belgica became part of the Roman Empire and experienced a period of economic prosperity and urbanization. The Romans built roads, bridges and aqueducts that crisscrossed the country and promoted mobility and trade. Cities such as Trier (Augusta Treverorum) and Tongeren (Atuatuca Tungrorum) became important centres of administration and trade in the region.

The Romans also introduced their culture and religion to the region. Temples, baths, and amphitheaters were built, and Roman mythology and philosophy influenced daily life. The spread of Christianity also began during this period, although it was initially met with skepticism and only later gained importance.

However, the Roman presence in Gallia Belgica was not without conflicts. Germanic tribes such as the Eburones, led by Ambiorix, rose up against

Roman rule and led the famous Eburones Revolt in 54 BC. This revolt was brutally suppressed by the Romans.

The Roman period in Gallia Belgica lasted until the 5th century AD, when the Roman Empire collapsed in the west and the region was conquered by Germanic tribes. This marked the end of Roman rule and the beginning of a new era for Belgium.

The Roman period in the history of Belgium was characterized by a mixture of cultural takeover and local resistance. The traces of this era can still be seen today in the archaeological remains, the ancient cities and the historical artifacts that bear witness to a time when Belgium was part of the mighty Roman Empire.

The Franks and the birth of Belgium

The Frankish era marked a decisive turning point in the history of Belgium and its emergence as an independent territory. The Franks, a Germanic people, played a crucial role in the transformation of the region, which had previously been ruled by the Romans.

In the 5th century AD, after the collapse of the Western Roman Empire, the Franks began to infiltrate the region and gradually settle. Their influence grew over time, and they established the Frankish Empire, which stretched over large parts of Europe. Belgium, then part of Gallia Belgica, was integrated into this empire.

An important moment in the history of Belgium was the baptism of the Frankish King Clovis I in 496. He converted to Christianity and led the Franks to adopt Christianity as the state religion. This had not only religious, but also political consequences, as the close relationship between the church and the Frankish kingdom promoted political stability.

Over the following centuries, the Frankish Empire continued to develop, and the region now known as Belgium was divided into different counties and duchies. The Frankish rulers, including the Carolingians and the Merovingians, exercised their rule over this area.

In the 9th and 10th centuries, Belgium experienced a certain political fragmentation, with local nobles expanding their power and creating independent dominions. This development laid the foundation for the later development of the country.

The birth of Belgium as an independent territory began in the High Middle Ages. In 1437, Philip the Good of Burgundy inherited the various Belgian counties and united them under his rule. Under his successor, Charles the Bold, the Duchy of Burgundy reached its greatest extent and extended into today's Netherlands and parts of France.

However, after the death of Charles the Bold in 1477, a War of Succession broke out, known as the Burgundian Wars. Eventually, the Belgian territories fell to the House of Habsburg, which led to a long period of Habsburg rule over Belgium.

The era of the Franks and the emergence of Belgium are closely linked. The influences of the Frankish kings and their successors have shaped the country and are an important part of its history. Belgium began to form itself as an independent political entity, and the developments of this period laid the foundation for the country's later development.

The Burgundian Rule and the Burgundian Netherlands

The period of Burgundian rule in the so-called Burgundian Netherlands was a decisive phase in the history of Belgium and the surrounding areas. It spanned the 15th century and was marked by political changes, cultural influences and economic boom.

The era began in 1369, when Philip the Bold of Burgundy inherited the County of Flanders and extended his power in the Belgian regions. Under his successors, including John the Fearless and Philip the Good, the Duchy of Burgundy experienced a period of expansion, during which they integrated other Belgian territories such as Brabant, Holland and Luxembourg into their territory.

Burgundian rule was characterized by an efficient administration and a policy of centralization. The Dukes of Burgundy sought to consolidate their control over the various Belgian regions and establish a strong central government. This led to the formation of the Burgundian Netherlands, a political entity consisting of a large number of counties and duchies and in its entirety as a unified entity under the rule of the duke.

The Burgundian rule also brought cultural flourishing and artistic developments. Court life in the cities of Brussels and Bruges was marked by pomp and splendour. Painting flourished, and famous artists such as Jan van Eyck created impressive works. The Flemish art school gained worldwide recognition.

Economically, the Burgundian Netherlands experienced an upswing, especially due to trade. The location on the North Sea and the well-developed trade routes led to lively trade with cities throughout Europe. Antwerp became an important trading centre and one of the most important ports in Europe.

Despite this period of prosperity, Burgundian rule was not without conflicts. In 1477, Charles the Bold died in the Burgundian War, and the Burgundian Netherlands fell to the House of Habsburg, leading to a new era of Habsburg rule.

The period of Burgundian rule and the emergence of the Burgundian Netherlands have had a significant influence on the history of Belgium and its neighbouring regions. This period was marked by political changes, cultural flourishing and economic boom and has shaped the country in many ways.

The Habsburgs and the Spanish Rule

The Habsburg era and the subsequent Spanish rule in the Belgian regions are of great importance for the history of Belgium and its political development. This period spanned a considerable period of time, from the late 15th century to the beginning of the 18th century, and brought profound changes and challenges.

The Habsburgs, a powerful European ruling house, took control of the Burgundian Netherlands after the death of Charles the Bold in 1477. Under Maximilian I, the Duchy of Burgundy was united with the Habsburg hereditary lands, which led to a stronger bond between the regions.

During the Habsburg rule, the Burgundian Netherlands was integrated into the Habsburg Empire, which was one of the most powerful dynasties in Europe at the time. Emperor Charles V, who ruled in the 16th century, was an important Habsburg who also ruled over large parts of Europe, including the Holy Roman Empire, Spain, and the New World.

However, this time was also marked by religious conflicts. The Reformation gained influence in the Belgian regions, which led to religious tensions. Under Charles V and later under his son Philip II, the Catholic Church was promoted as the state religion, which led to religious unrest and conflict.

In 1566, the so-called iconoclasm broke out, in which Reformation groups destroyed religious symbols in churches and monasteries. This led to a military response from Philip II, who ruled the duchies of Flanders and Brabant with a heavy hand. The brutal repression and persecution of Protestants eventually led to the Eighty Years' War, a long-lasting conflict between the Dutch rebels and the Spanish crown, which was controlled by the Habsburgs at the time.

The Eighty Years' War, which began in 1568, eventually led to the independence of the Netherlands in 1648, while the southern regions that now form Belgium remained under Spanish rule. These southern territories became known as the Spanish Netherlands and remained under Spanish rule until the end of the War of the Spanish Succession in 1713, when they passed to Austria and became part of the Habsburg Monarchy.

The Habsburg era and Spanish rule were marked by political upheavals, religious conflicts and social changes. This period left a lasting mark on the history of Belgium and laid the foundation for the country's later development as an independent nation.

The Belgian Revolution of 1830

The Belgian Revolution of 1830 marked a decisive turning point in the history of Belgium and led to the establishment of the independent Kingdom of Belgium. This revolution was the result of a multitude of political, social and economic factors that had built up over years.

At the beginning of the 19th century, Belgium was part of the United Kingdom of the Netherlands, which was under the rule of King William I. The unification of Belgium with the northern provinces that now form the Netherlands was the result of the Congress of Vienna in 1815, which regulated the territorial reorganization of Europe after the Napoleonic Wars.

However, unification proved difficult because the northern and southern provinces were culturally, linguistically and economically different. In the southern regions, including Flanders and Wallonia, French was preferred as the official language, while the northern provinces spoke Dutch. This led to tensions and discontent in the southern regions, which felt oppressed by the political dominance of the northern provinces.

Dissatisfaction grew over time, especially due to economic problems and rising taxes. The industrial revolution had begun, and the southern regions felt disadvantaged, as they benefited less from economic progress than the northern provinces.

The spark that ignited the Belgian Revolution was the performance of the opera "La Muette de Portici" at the La Monnaie Opera House in Brussels on August 25, 1830. The opera was about a popular uprising in Naples against the rule of the Bourbons and encouraged the audience to rise up against Dutch rule. This led to riots and riots that quickly spread to other cities.

On October 4, 1830, the insurgents in Brussels officially declared their independence from the Netherlands and proclaimed the birth of the independent state of Belgium. The revolutionaries drafted a constitution and looked for a suitable monarch who would recognize their independence.

Eventually, Leopold of Saxe-Coburg-Gotha, a German prince, was appointed King of Belgium and accepted the Belgian crown in July 1831. This led to international recognition of Belgium's independence, although it took a few years for final recognition by the great powers to take place.

The Belgian Revolution of 1830 led to the founding of the modern Kingdom of Belgium and the establishment of an independent nation. This revolution was an important event in the history of Belgium and laid the foundation for the political and cultural development of the country in the decades that followed.

The Emergence of Modern Belgium

The emergence of modern Belgium is a fascinating chapter in the history of Europe, marked by a complex sequence of political, cultural and historical events. After the Belgian Revolution of 1830 and the Declaration of Independence, the foundation was laid for the emergence of an independent and sovereign state of Belgium.

The proclamation of Belgium's independence in 1830 was a decisive step towards an independent state. The Congress of National Deputies proclaimed separation from the United Netherlands on October 4, 1830, and the Declaration of Independence was signed on October 4, 1830.

The search for a suitable monarch led to the election of Leopold of Saxe-Coburg-Gotha as King of Belgium. He accepted the crown in 1831 and became the first monarch of modern Belgium. Leopold's acceptance by the major European powers contributed to the international recognition of Belgian independence.

The drafting of a constitution was an important step on the way to the founding of modern Belgium. The Constitution of 1831 laid down the basic principles of the new state, including the separation of powers, freedom of religion and the rights of citizens. It also created a constitutional monarchy in which the king played a symbolic role and legislative power rested with parliament.

One of the biggest challenges for young Belgium was the question of nationality and languages. The country was multilingual from the beginning, with Dutch, French and German as official languages. The linguistic and cultural differences between the regions led to tensions that can still be felt in Belgian politics today.

In the course of the 19th century and the early 20th century, Belgium developed into a modern industrial state. The Industrial Revolution brought economic progress, especially in the regions of Flanders and Wallonia. The Belgian economy prospered, and the country became an important trading center in Europe.

The two world wars of the 20th century had a significant impact on Belgium. The country became an important battlefield in the First World War and suffered heavy losses. During World War II, Belgium was occupied by German troops and experienced a period of oppression and resistance.

After World War II, Belgium became a founding member of the European Union and NATO. The country played an important role in European integration and is now the headquarters of numerous international organizations.

The emergence of modern Belgium was a complex and historically significant process. Since its inception, the country has developed into a diverse and multicultural nation that plays an important role in Europe and the world. Belgium's history is marked by political stability, economic boom and cultural diversity, and it contributes to Europe's rich cultural and historical landscape.

Belgium in the First World War

The First World War, which lasted from 1914 to 1918, had a far-reaching impact on Belgium and its people. The country, which was neutral at the beginning of the war, soon became the scene of devastating fighting and the victim of German aggression.

On August 4, 1914, the German Empire violated Belgian neutrality and crossed the borders of Belgium on its way to France. This triggered an international crisis and led to the British declaration of war on Germany, as Britain had signed an agreement to defend Belgian neutrality.

The Belgian army put up brave resistance to the German superiority, but could not prevent large parts of the country from being conquered by the Germans. The Battle of Liège, in which Belgian forts fought against the German troops, marked the beginning of the invasion. The city of Leuven was heavily bombed, and the Belgian army retreated to the west.

The resistance of the Belgian civilian population against the German occupation was strong, and an underground resistance was formed. Belgians, who fought as civilians, defended themselves against the German occupiers, and acts of sabotage were often carried out.

One of the most tragic consequences of the war was the destruction of towns and villages and the loss of life. Belgium became a battlefield, and the destruction was far-reaching. The regions of Flanders and Wallonia in particular suffered from the devastation of the war.

The First World War also brought a humanitarian crisis, as the civilian population suffered from food shortages and mistreatment by the occupiers. Many Belgians were deported or forced to do forced labor.

The war ended in November 1918, when the Allies were able to defeat the German troops. Belgium regained its independence, and the Treaty of Versailles confirmed the country's borders. However, the Belgian population and infrastructure had paid a high price.

The First World War left deep traces in the history of Belgium. The country had fought bravely against the German invasion and suffered heavy losses. The experiences of the war and the destruction left their mark on Belgian society and had a long-term impact on the country's national identity and political development.

Belgium in World War II

The Second World War, which lasted from 1939 to 1945, again had a serious impact on Belgium and its population. However, the country, which once again wanted to remain neutral, was once again gripped by the violence of war when the German Wehrmacht invaded Belgium in May 1940.

The German invasion of Belgium and the Battle of Belgium in May 1940 led to the rapid conquest of the country. The Belgian army fought bravely, but the German superiority in terms of troop strength and technology was overwhelming. The Belgian government, under King Leopold III, capitulated on May 28, 1940.

During the German occupation, Belgium was subject to the authoritarian control of the Third Reich. The occupiers carried out a policy of oppression and exploitation and forced the Belgian population to do forced labour. Many Belgians were deported to Germany to work in the war industry.

The Holocaust also had a devastating impact on Belgium. The Jewish population was persecuted, deported and murdered. The Mechelen deportation camp served as a collection camp for

Jewish prisoners, who were then deported to concentration camps in the east.

Belgian resistance to the German occupation was strong, and underground movements were formed, carrying out acts of sabotage and gathering information for the Allies. The Battle of the Bulge of 1944, a German attempt to push back the Allies, took place partly on Belgian soil and led to heavy fighting and destruction.

The liberation of Belgium began in September 1944, when Allied troops crossed the Ardennes and repelled the German occupation. The cities of Brussels and Antwerp were liberated in the autumn of 1944, and the German Wehrmacht withdrew from Belgium.

The Second World War left deep wounds in Belgium. The destruction and losses were enormous, and the experiences of the war shaped Belgian society and politics in the years that followed. Participation in international organisations such as the United Nations and the European Union was a response to the lessons of the wars of the 20th century and a contribution to the promotion of peace and cooperation in Europe and the world.

The European Union and Belgium

The relationship between Belgium and the European Union (EU) is fundamental and has a long history. Belgium was one of the founding members of the European Coal and Steel Community (ECSC) in 1951 and played a crucial role in the creation of the European Economic Community (EEC) and the European Atomic Energy Community (Euratom) in 1957. These communities formed the forerunner of today's European Union.

The Belgian capital, Brussels, is also home to the main EU institutions, including the European Commission, the Council of the European Union, and the European Parliament. This makes Belgium a key player in European politics and administration.

Belgium has played an active role in the EU over the years, promoting European integration and cooperation. The country has co-signed and supported the various EU treaties and reforms. It has also hosted numerous EU summits and international negotiations.

The EU has a significant influence on the daily lives of Belgian citizens. The open border and the common internal market allow for smooth trade and the free movement of persons. The euro is the official currency of Belgium and many other EU countries.

EU funds and programmes support projects in Belgium, from infrastructure funding to research funding. Belgium also benefits from EU directives and regulations in areas such as environmental protection, consumer protection and labour law.

The European Union also provides a platform for Belgium to act at international level and defend its own interests. The country is a member of various EU bodies and committees that influence political decisions and developments in Europe.

Despite this close relationship, there are also challenges and tensions between Belgium and the EU. The issue of Belgian regionalisation and the responsibilities of federal and regional governments within Belgium have implications for the implementation of EU legislation.

Overall, the relationship between Belgium and the European Union remains of great importance and shapes the political, economic and social landscape of the country. Belgium will continue to play an important role in the EU and benefit from European integration, while defending its own interests and values in the Union.

Belgian kings and the monarchy

The Belgian monarchy has a long and eventful history, which is closely linked to the development of the country. Since Belgium's independence in 1830, there has been a continuous line of Belgian kings ruling the country.

Leopold I was appointed the first king of the Belgians in 1831 and was a German prince from the House of Saxe-Coburg and Gotha. He accepted the crown and played an important role in establishing the Belgian monarchy in the early years of the nation.

Leopold I was succeeded by his son Leopold II, who reigned from 1865 to 1909. During his rule, Belgium gained international recognition and actively participated in the colonization of the Congo, a controversial period in Belgian history.

Albert I succeeded Leopold II to the throne in 1909 and became known as the "King-Soldier" during the First World War, as he personally fought at the front and led the Belgian people in a time of great need.

His son Leopold III took over in 1934, but his controversial role during World War II and his marriage to Lilian Baels, which was criticized by many, led to political tensions and eventually his abdication in 1951 in favor of his son Baudouin.

King Baudouin reigned from 1951 until his death in 1993 and was known for his moral integrity and social justice efforts. His brother, Albert II, succeeded him to the throne and was King of the Belgians from 1993 to 2013.

The current Belgian monarch is King Philippe, who took over the crown in 2013. He is married to Mathilde and has four children.

The Belgian monarchy has played a developed role over the years, which has evolved from a political to a symbolic monarchy. The kings and queens of Belgium have promoted national unity and shaped the country's identity.

The Belgian monarchy remains an important part of Belgium's political and cultural landscape. The royal family plays a representative role and represents the country on an international level. The monarchy is appreciated by many Belgians and contributes to the stability and unity of the country.

The Belgian Constitution and Politics

The Belgian Constitution is the fundamental legal document of the Kingdom of Belgium and defines the structure and functioning of the country. It was first adopted in 1831 and has since undergone several revisions and changes to meet the political developments and needs of the country.

Belgium is a federal monarchy and consists of three regions: Flanders, Wallonia and the Brussels-Capital Region. Each region has its own government with responsibilities in education, culture, transport and other regional affairs. The Brussels-Capital Region is an independent region with a special status and also functions as the capital of the European Union.

The federal government of Belgium is made up of various federal institutions, including the Federal Prime Minister, the Federal Council of Ministers, and the Federal Parliament. The federal parliament consists of two chambers: the Chamber of Deputies and the Senate. The Chamber of Deputies is the main legislative body in the country and consists of 150 elected deputies. The Senate has an advisory role and represents the different parts of the country.

Belgium also has a royal family that performs symbolic and representative tasks. The king or queen has no political power and acts on the recommendation of the elected government.

Belgian politics is characterised by a complex system of coalition building at federal and regional level. Since the country is made up of different regions with different political parties, the formation of coalition governments is necessary to achieve a majority in parliament.

Belgium's political landscape is diverse, with numerous political parties, including liberal, socialist, conservative, and green parties. The parties represent different political ideologies and interests.

Belgium also hosts international institutions, including the European Union and NATO, which plays an important role in the country's foreign policy.

The Belgian constitution and politics are characterised by federal structures, a complex political landscape and the need to compromise. Despite these challenges, Belgium has a stable democracy and plays an important role in European politics and diplomacy.

The education system in Belgium

The education system in Belgium is organised on a federal basis and is under the jurisdiction of the country's three regions: Flanders, Wallonia and the Brussels-Capital Region. Each of these regions has its own education system and policy, which leads to a certain diversity and autonomy in educational management.

In Belgium, education is compulsory for children aged 6 to 18. The education system is divided into different levels, starting with primary education, which usually lasts six years. Primary education is compulsory and free of charge and lays the foundations in mathematics, languages, natural sciences and social subjects.

Primary education is followed by secondary education, which is also compulsory in Belgium and usually lasts six years. Secondary education is divided into three cycles: the first cycle (1st and 2nd year), the second cycle (3rd and 4th year) and the third cycle (5th and 6th year). In secondary school, students choose a field of study that matches their interests and abilities, whether it is general, technical or vocational.

Belgium has a wide range of colleges and universities, usually funded by the communities. There are both Dutch-speaking and French-speaking universities in Belgium, which reflects the country's multilingualism. Higher education is largely free or accessible at low tuition fees, and Belgium has a long tradition of promoting education and research.

Education policy in Belgium is decentralized, which means that each region has the power to set its own educational goals, curricula, and educational reforms. This leads to certain differences in the education system between regions, with Flanders and Wallonia having their own education ministries and systems.

Belgium's multilingualism is also reflected in the education system. In Dutch-speaking schools, Dutch is used as the language of instruction, while in French-speaking schools, French is the main language. The Brussels-Capital Region offers schools in both languages to meet the needs of the international and multilingual population.

The education system in Belgium places great emphasis on the promotion of language skills, as multilingualism is an important part of Belgian culture and society. The promotion of education and research is a central concern of Belgian policy and contributes to economic development and innovation in the country.

Economy and trade in Belgium

Belgium has a diverse and stable economy, which is closely linked to its geographical location in Europe and its historical role as a trading nation. The country has a highly developed economy that is characterized by various industries.

One of the most important pillars of the Belgian economy is international trade. Belgium is located in the heart of Europe and has world-class ports such as Antwerp and Zeebrugge, which are among the largest in Europe. These ports serve as important entry and exit points for the movement of goods and international trade. Belgium is an important transshipment point for goods from all over the world and plays a crucial role in global trade.

The Belgian economy is also characterised by a strong industry. The automotive industry, chemical industry, food processing and mechanical engineering industry are some of the important sectors. Belgium is known for its high-quality products and its ability to innovate in various industries.

The service sector is also an important part of the Belgian economy. Financial services, healthcare, tourism and information and communication technology (ICT) are important areas that contribute to value creation and employment in the country.

Belgium has a stable and well-developed social market economy, characterised by a strong trade union movement and social security systems. The country has a high level of social security and a high quality of life for its citizens.

The Belgian economy is also strongly international. Belgium is a member of the European Union and the Eurozone, which means that the euro is the country's official currency. This facilitates trade and economic integration in Europe.

Despite its economic strength, Belgium also faces some challenges. The country's high level of public debt and complex political structure can have an impact on economic performance. The burden of taxes and social security contributions is also high.

However, the Belgian economy remains robust and diverse. The country has a long tradition of trade and industry and relies on innovation and research to remain competitive. Belgium plays an important role in the European economy and is an attractive destination for investors from all over the world.

Belgian architecture and art

Over the centuries, Belgium has developed a rich and diverse architectural and artistic tradition, which is reflected in different eras and styles. Belgian architecture and art are of historical significance and have shaped the country's cultural heritage.

One of Belgium's most important architectural achievements is undoubtedly the Grand-Place in Brussels. This historic market square is surrounded by magnificent 17th-century buildings built in the Flemish Baroque style. The Grand-Place is considered one of the most beautiful squares in Europe and was declared a World Heritage Site by UNESCO in 1998.

Another outstanding example of Belgian architecture is the Atomium, a futuristic building in Brussels built for the 1958 Expo. A symbol of scientific progress and technological innovation, the Atomium attracts thousands of tourists every year.

Belgian architecture is also characterized by its medieval towns and castles. Cities such as Bruges and Ghent have well-preserved medieval old towns with impressive churches, town halls and belfries. Gravensteen Castle in Ghent is an impressive example of a medieval castle that takes visitors back in time to the country's history.

In the Renaissance period, Belgian artists played an important role in the European art scene. Pieter Bruegel the Elder, a famous Flemish painter, created detailed paintings depicting rural life and customs of his time. His work "The Peasant Wedding Dance" is a well-known example of this.

The Flemish Primitives, a group of painters of the 15th century, contributed to the development of oil painting and left behind masterpieces such as the "Ghent Altarpiece" by Jan van Eyck. These artists had a lasting influence on European painting.

In the 20th century, Belgium was a center for the development of surrealism in art. Artists such as René Magritte created mysterious and fascinating works that explored the boundaries of reality and the subconscious.

The Belgian art scene remains vibrant and innovative, with contemporary artists gaining international recognition. Belgium is also home to numerous museums and galleries, including the Royal Museum of Fine Arts in Brussels and the MAS Museum in Antwerp.

Belgian architecture and art are an integral part of the country's culture and heritage. They reflect the history, diversity and creativity of Belgium and are an important aspect of its identity in the world of art and architecture.

The rich tradition of Belgian comics

Belgium has a remarkable and globally recognized tradition in the field of comics. Often referred to as the "Ninth Art", this art form has a long history in Belgium and has had a significant influence on pop culture and the art world.

The origin of Belgian comics can be traced back to the early 20th century, when illustrators such as Hergé and his famous character Tintin (Tintin in the original) first appeared. Tintin is probably the most famous Belgian comic book characters and has conquered a worldwide fan base. Hergé's precise drawings, exciting adventures and humorous stories have helped to establish the reputation of Belgian comics.

Another outstanding Belgian comic artist is Peyo, the creator of the Smurfs (Les Schtroumpfs in the original). These little blue creatures have become pop culture icons and have inspired their own comics, TV series, and movies.

There is also a wide range of comics in Belgium, covering different genres and topics. The adventures of Spirou and Fantasio, the humorous stories of Gaston Lagaffe, the realistic works of André Franquin and the fantastic worlds of Jean-Claude Mézières are just a few examples of the diversity and creativity of the Belgian comic scene.

Belgian comics are also known for their high artistic quality and sophisticated stories. Illustrators such as Moebius and François Schuiten have pushed the boundaries of comic art and created innovative works that are recognized as works of art.

The Belgian capital, Brussels, is home to the Comic Strip Centre (Centre Belge de la Bande Dessinée), a museum and research facility dedicated to the history and development of comics. The Comic Center is a popular destination for comic book lovers from all over the world.

The Belgian comic tradition has also had a strong influence on the European and international comic scene. Numerous Belgian artists have received prizes and awards for their work and are recognized as pioneers and masters of the medium.

Overall, the Belgian comic scene is characterised by creativity, innovation and artistic excellence. It has a long tradition that is still alive today and continues to produce new talent. The rich world of Belgian comics remains a fascinating and inspiring facet of Belgium's cultural landscape.

The role of Belgium in world literature

Belgium has made a significant contribution to world literature over the centuries and has produced some outstanding writers who have achieved international fame. The Belgian literary scene is diverse and reflects the linguistic diversity of the country, as there are both Dutch- and French-speaking writers.

One of the most famous Belgian authors of the 19th century was Charlotte Brontë. Although she was born in England, she spent part of her life in Belgium and processed her experiences in her novel "Villette". This work is an important contribution to English literature and shows the influence of Belgium on the works of foreign writers.

In the field of French-language literature, Belgium is particularly known for its Symbolist movement. Symbolist poets such as Emile Verhaeren and Maurice Maeterlinck shaped the literary world of the late 19th century. Maeterlinck was awarded the Nobel Prize for Literature in 1911 and his work "Pelléas et Mélisande" is one of the most important works of French literature.

Another important Belgian writer is Georges Simenon, who is best known for his crime novels about Inspector Maigret. Simenon's works have been translated into numerous languages and have inspired millions of readers worldwide.

Belgian literature is also characterised by its Dutch-speaking authors. Among the most famous are Hendrik Conscience, who is considered the "father of Flemish literature", and Hugo Claus, a versatile writer who was successful in various genres.

The diversity of Belgian literature ranges from novels and poems to plays and essays. Belgian authors have covered a wide range of topics, including love, society, politics, and existential issues. Their works often reflect the cultural and linguistic diversity of the country.

Belgium also has a vibrant contemporary literary scene, with internationally acclaimed authors such as Amélie Nothomb, Dimitri Verhulst and Stefan Hertmans. Her works deal with current social and cultural issues and contribute to further shaping the image of Belgium in world literature.

Overall, Belgium has a rich literary tradition that is characterized by different languages, styles, and genres. Belgian literature has gained national and international recognition and contributes to the country's cultural diversity and heritage.

The Belgian music scene

The Belgian music scene is extremely diverse and has produced a wide range of musical styles and artists throughout history that have enjoyed success both nationally and internationally. Belgium has exerted a significant influence on the European music landscape and is known for its creative and innovative music scene.

In classical music, Belgium has produced some outstanding composers and musicians. César Franck, a Belgian composer of the 19th century, is famous for his romantic works and his organ playing. The violinist Eugène Ysaÿe is one of the most important violinists of his time and was a pioneer in the interpretation of violin music.

The Belgian opera scene has also achieved international success. Soprano Joséphine-Charlotte of Belgium and tenor Jules Bastin are just a few examples of talented opera singers who hail from Belgium and have performed on the world's most prestigious stages.

In pop and rock music, Belgium has produced a vibrant scene with many influential bands and artists. One of the most famous Belgian bands is dEUS, which achieved international breakthrough in the 1990s. Their 1999 album

"The Ideal Crash" is often considered a masterpiece of alternative rock.

Another successful Belgian band is Hooverphonic, known for their unique sound and captivating live performances. Their hit "Mad About You" from 2000 earned them international recognition.

The electronic music scene in Belgium also has a significant influence on dance music worldwide. Belgian DJs and producers such as Dimitri Vegas & Like Mike, Lost Frequencies and Charlotte de Witte are highly regarded in the electronic music scene and have enjoyed great success at international festivals and clubs.

The Belgian music scene is also known for its diversity. It includes jazz, hip-hop, rap, chanson, and many other genres. Artists such as Jacques Brel, who is considered one of the greatest chansonniers of the 20th century, have shaped the Belgian music scene.

Belgium also has an active and emerging indie music scene, which produces many talented young artists. The diversity and openness of the Belgian music scene reflect the cultural diversity and cosmopolitanism of the country.

In conclusion, the Belgian music scene is rich in talent and diversity. It has made many significant contributions to the international musical landscape throughout history and remains an important cultural facet of Belgium. The country's musicians and artists use their creative energy and talent to inspire and enrich the world with their music.

Religion and Spirituality in Belgium

Belgium is a country that is shaped by a variety of religious traditions and a wide range of spiritual beliefs. The religious landscape in Belgium reflects the cultural and historical diversity of the country and has undergone various developments over the centuries.

The dominant religion in Belgium is Christianity, with the Roman Catholic Church being the largest Christian denomination. The Catholic Church has a long history in Belgium and played a significant role in the country's culture and society. Belgium is divided into dioceses, and the cathedrals of Brussels, Antwerp and Liège are important religious centres.

In addition to Catholicism, there is also a significant Protestant community in Belgium, as well as Orthodox, Anglican and other Christian denominations. This diversity reflects the country's religious tolerance and offers believers a wide range of spiritual experiences.

In addition, Belgium has a growing Muslim community, mainly due to immigration in recent decades. Mosques and Islamic centers can be found in various cities across the country, and Islam has become an important religious community.

The Jewish community in Belgium also has a long history and is now present in cities such as Antwerp and Brussels. Synagogues and Jewish community centers serve as places of prayer and gathering.

In addition to organized religions, there is also a growing number of people in Belgium who consider themselves non-religious or agnostic. Humanism and secular ethics have gained prominence in Belgian society, and many people seek their spiritual fulfillment outside traditional religious structures.

The diversity of religious and spiritual beliefs in Belgium is also reflected in the numerous religious holidays and festivals celebrated in the country. These festivals are often opportunities for meeting and exchange between the different communities and contribute to the cultural diversity of the country.

Overall, Belgium is a country where religious freedom is respected, and the diversity of spiritual beliefs and practices enriches the country's cultural landscape. Religion and spirituality are important aspects of the lives of the people of Belgium and contribute to shaping their identity and social cohesion.

Brussels: The capital of Europe

Brussels, the capital of Belgium, is at the same time the political heart of Europe and the seat of many international organizations. The city has a rich history dating back to Roman times and has become an important political and cultural center over the centuries.

One of Brussels' most striking sights is the Atomium, a futuristic building built for the 1958 World's Fair. It symbolizes the pursuit of scientific progress and has become a landmark of the city.

The Grand-Place, the central market square of Brussels, is another highlight. With its magnificent 17th-century Baroque buildings, it is a UNESCO World Heritage Site and an impressive example of European architecture.

Brussels is also known for its culinary delights, especially chocolate and Belgian beer. The city is home to numerous chocolate shops where visitors can sample the finest chocolate in the world. Belgian beer culture is also remarkable, and a variety of breweries offer a wide range of beers, from lambic to Trappist beer.

The city is home to the European Quarter, where most of the EU institutions are located. The

European Parliament, the European Commission and the European Council are based in Brussels, making the city the political centre of the European Union.

In addition to its political importance, Brussels also has cultural diversity to offer. The city is bilingual, with French and Dutch as official languages. This is reflected in the cultural scene, where theatre, music and art flourish in both languages.

Museums in Brussels are diverse, ranging from classical art at the Royal Museum of Fine Arts to modern art at the Magritte Museum, dedicated to surrealist painter René Magritte.

Brussels is a city that combines the past and the present. Its history and culture, its culinary delights and its political significance make it a fascinating place that attracts visitors from all over the world. As the capital of Europe, Brussels plays a central role in global politics while remaining a place of cultural diversity and creativity.

Antwerp: The diamond city

Antwerp, the largest city in Flanders and the capital of the province of Antwerp, is known far beyond the country's borders for its importance in the diamond trade and its rich cultural history.

The history of Antwerp dates back to the Middle Ages, when the city became an important trading center in Europe. Its port, one of the largest in Europe, played a crucial role in the trade of goods from all over the world. Antwerp became a melting pot of cultures and nations, resulting in a thriving artistic and economic scene.

The city was home to famous artists such as Peter Paul Rubens, one of the most important painters of the Baroque. The Rubens House, now a museum, is an impressive example of the architecture of the period and houses an extensive collection of his works.

Antwerp also has a rich religious history and is known for its magnificent churches, including Antwerp Cathedral, a Gothic church with an imposing tower. The city has a strong Catholic tradition, which is reflected in its historic churches and processions.

However, what has made Antwerp famous worldwide is the diamond trade. The city has a long tradition of processing and trading diamonds and is considered the diamond capital of the world. The Diamond District, also known as the "Diamond District," is the center of this industry and is home to numerous diamond dealers, cutters and jewelers.

The diamond trade in Antwerp dates back to the 15th century and has made the city a world-leading centre for diamonds. Here, diamonds are cut, graded and resold, and the city attracts jewelers and customers from all over the world.

The importance of the diamond trade is also reflected in the security that prevails in Antwerp. The diamond district is strictly secured, and the transport of diamonds is extremely carefully monitored.

However, Antwerp is not only known for diamonds and art, but also for its diverse culinary scene. The city is famous for its Belgian chocolate, Belgian beer and fries. The cosy cafés and restaurants offer a wide range of food and drinks that celebrate Belgian food culture.

In summary, Antwerp is a city that combines history, culture, business and enjoyment. Its role in the diamond trade, its cultural heritage and its gastronomic diversity make it a fascinating destination for travellers and an important centre in Flanders and Europe.

Ghent: The charming city of art

Ghent, also known as "Ghent" in Flemish, is one of the most fascinating and charming cities in Belgium. Located in the Flanders region, the city has a rich history that is reflected in its architecture, art, and culture.

One of the most striking sights in Ghent is the Gravensteen, also known as the "Castle of the Counts". This imposing medieval castle was built in the 12th century and once served as a fortress and residence of the Counts of Flanders. Today, the Gravensteen is an impressive example of medieval architecture and a popular tourist destination.

Ghent is also known for its well-preserved medieval buildings and canals, which give the city a unique atmosphere. Ghent's canals are lined with historic buildings and are a reminder of the city's rich past as a trading centre in the Middle Ages.

St. Bavo's Cathedral is another impressive sight in Ghent. It houses the famous altarpiece "The Adoration of the Mystical Lamb" by Jan van Eyck, one of the most important works of Flemish painting. The cathedral itself is a masterpiece of Gothic architecture.

Ghent also has a vibrant art scene, which is reflected in the city's numerous galleries and art exhibitions. The city has a long tradition of promoting art and culture and is home to many talented artists and artisans.

The University of Ghent, one of the oldest universities in Europe, contributes to the intellectual and cultural vitality of the city. It has a long history of research and education, attracting students from all over the world.

The culinary scene in Ghent is characterised by Belgian specialities such as moules-frites (mussels with French fries), waffles and Belgian beer. The city's cozy restaurants and cafes offer a wide range of taste experiences that celebrate Belgian food culture.

Ghent is also known for its numerous markets selling fresh food, antiques and handicrafts. The Flower Market, Friday Market, and Bird Market are just a few examples of the city's vibrant markets.

In summary, Ghent is a city that combines history, art, culture and enjoyment in an enchanting setting. Its medieval roots, vibrant art scene and culinary delights make it a unique destination in Belgium and a place that visitors want to discover again and again. Ghent is undoubtedly a charming city of art to explore.

Bruges: The "Venice of the North"

Bruges, often referred to as the "Venice of the North", is one of the best-preserved medieval cities in Europe and a true gem in Belgium. The city is located in the Flanders region and has a rich history, which is reflected in its architecture, culture, and romantic atmosphere.

One of the most striking sights in Bruges is the medieval market square known as the "Grote Markt". This impressive square is lined with historic buildings, including the Gothic Town Hall and the Belfry. The Belfry of Bruges is an imposing tower that once served as a bell tower and city gate and is now a UNESCO World Heritage Site.

The canals of Bruges are another characteristic feature of the city and are reminiscent of Venice. The canal cruises offer visitors a unique perspective on the historic architecture and picturesque streets of Bruges.

St. Salvator's Cathedral and St. James' Church are impressive religious buildings in Bruges that are home to a rich history and beautiful works of art. The cathedral is also home to an impressive collection of artwork, including paintings and sculptures.

Bruges is known for its lace-making, a traditional craft that has been practiced here for centuries. The lace from Bruges is famous worldwide for its fine quality and detailed craftsmanship.

The city also has a rich culinary scene that celebrates Belgian specialties such as chocolate, waffles, and Belgian beer. The numerous restaurants and cafes offer visitors the opportunity to taste these delicacies and enjoy Belgian hospitality.

Bruges is also a popular destination for art lovers, as the city is home to a variety of museums and galleries. The Groeninge Museum houses an impressive collection of Flemish masterpieces, including works by Jan van Eyck and Hieronymus Bosch.

The romantic atmosphere of Bruges has made the city a popular destination for honeymooners. The narrow streets, historic buildings and idyllic canals create an enchanting backdrop for lovers.

In summary, Bruges is a truly unique destination that combines history, architecture, art and romance in an enchanting setting. The city has rightly earned its nickname as the "Venice of the North" and remains a place that visitors want to discover again and again due to its beauty and historical heritage. Bruges is undoubtedly an enchanting gem in Belgium to explore.

Liège: an industrial city with a history

Liège, also known as Liège in French, is a city in Belgium that offers a fascinating mix of industrial history and cultural diversity. Located in Wallonia, the French-speaking region of Belgium, the city has undergone impressive development over the centuries.

The history of Liège dates back to Roman times, when the city was an important trading city. Later, it became an important center for the metal industry and mining. This industrial development shaped the city and led to its reputation as an "industrial city".

One of the most eye-catching sights in Liège is the Palais des Princes-Évêques, an impressive Baroque building that once served as the residence of the prince-bishops of Liège. The palace now houses the State Archives and is a testimony to the historical importance of the city.

Liège Cathedral, also known as St. Paul's Cathedral, is another significant religious building in the city. It is an example of Gothic architecture and houses valuable religious artifacts.

Liège also has a vibrant cultural scene. The city is known for its festivals and events, including the

"Festival International du Film Francophone de Namur" and the "Les Ardentes" music festival. The University of Liège is an important educational institution and contributes to the cultural diversity of the city.

Liège's local cuisine is hearty and hearty, with dishes such as boulets à la liégeoise (meatballs in sauce) and gaufres de liège (Liège waffles) being popular. The city is also known for its beer, including the famous "Boulevard" beer.

Liège has a long history of social movements and trade unions that emerged in the industrial era. These movements have shaped the city and its inhabitants have often campaigned for social justice and workers' rights.

However, the city also has its challenges, including economic change and social inequality. In recent years, however, Liège has made efforts to revitalize the city and improve the quality of life for its residents.

In summary, Liège is a city with a rich history and a diverse cultural scene. Its industrial past has shaped the city, but it remains a place that combines history, culture and social changes. Liège is a city that deserves to be discovered and explored to understand its unique history and dynamism.

The Ardennes: Belgium's natural paradise

The Ardennes, a vast forest area in southeastern Belgium, is a true natural paradise and a popular destination for nature lovers and outdoor enthusiasts. This area also extends into the neighbouring countries of Luxembourg and France and offers a breathtaking variety of landscapes and leisure opportunities.

The characteristic feature of the Ardennes is its dense forests, rolling hills and deep valleys. The region is rich in natural beauty and offers numerous opportunities for activities such as hiking, cycling, climbing and fishing. The forests are crossed by numerous rivers and streams, including the Meuse and the Ourthe, which wind through picturesque gorges.

An outstanding natural area in the Ardennes is the High Fens-Eifel Nature Park, a protected raised bog and a unique landscape of international importance. The raised bog extends over wide areas and is characterized by unique flora and fauna, including rare plants and birds.

The Ardennes are also known for their spectacular caves and grottoes. The caves of Han-sur-Lesse are one of the most remarkable examples and offer visitors the opportunity to explore the underground world. The stalactite formations and impressive cave rooms are fascinating and tell of the geological history of the region.

The Ardennes are a paradise for wildlife watching. The dense forests are home to a variety of animal species, including deer, wild boar, foxes, and badgers. The region is also home to rare bird species such as the black stork and the rough-legged buzzard.

The small picturesque villages and towns in the Ardennes are charming and offer the opportunity to experience Belgian hospitality and local cuisine. The region is known for its hearty dishes, including game dishes, trout from the rivers and traditional cheeses.

The Ardennes is not only a popular destination in summer, but also offers numerous activities in winter. Skiing and snowboarding in the Ardennes is popular with locals and tourists alike, and the region offers several ski resorts and trails.

In summary, the Ardennes is a natural paradise in Belgium that offers a wealth of outdoor activities, breathtaking landscapes and cultural treasures. The region is a retreat for nature lovers and a place of relaxation and discovery. The Ardennes are undoubtedly a jewel in Belgium's nature and invite you to explore the beauty and diversity of this unique area.

The flora and fauna of Belgium

Belgium, a small country in Western Europe, is home to an amazing variety of flora and fauna shaped by its diverse landscapes and ecosystems. Despite its limited geographical size, Belgium offers a rich natural environment, ranging from the coast on the North Sea to the Ardennes in the southeast.

The Belgian coast is home to extensive sandy beaches and dunes, which are characterised by unique coastal flora. The dunes are home to plant species such as beach grass and sea mustard, which are adapted to the harsh conditions of coastal life. The sandy beaches are also habitat for various species of birds, including seagulls and shorebirds.

In the interior of Belgium, especially in the Ardennes, there are dense forests, rolling hills and deep valleys. This region is a refuge for a variety of animal species, including deer, wild boar, foxes, badgers and hares. The forests are crisscrossed by numerous streams and rivers that are home to trout and other fish species.

The Ardennes are also home to birds of prey such as the peregrine falcon and the sparrowhawk, which hunt in the forests and gorges. The region is rich in natural caves inhabited by bats, including the Great Net Cave System, which is considered one of the largest in Europe.

Belgium also has a rich birdlife, ranging from waterfowl on the river banks to songbirds in the forests. The Belgian coastal areas are an important habitat for waders and migratory birds that stop off on their journeys between Europe and Africa.

In the flat, fertile areas of Flanders and Wallonia, there are numerous agricultural areas where cereals, fruit and vegetables are grown. The rivers and canals in these regions are home to a variety of fish species, including pike and carp.

The flora of Belgium is characterized by forests, meadows and gardens. Various tree species grow in the forests of the Ardennes, such as beech, oak, pine and fir. In spring, wild flowers such as the wood anemone and the chess flower bloom, bathing the forests in bright colors.

Belgium also has a rich tradition of horticulture, with numerous botanical gardens and parks showcasing the diversity of plant life. The Royal Serres of Laeken, the Royal Greenhouses of Brussels, are an impressive example of exotic plants and palm trees that thrive in a magnificent glasshouse.

In conclusion, despite being a small country, Belgium offers a remarkable variety of flora and fauna. The country's diverse landscapes and ecosystems provide habitats for a wide range of animal and plant species. The protection and care of these natural resources are essential to preserve the diversity of Belgian nature for future generations.

Belgian beers: a world of their own

Belgium has earned a worldwide reputation as the home of some of the best beers in the world. Belgian beer culture is rich, diverse and deeply rooted in the country's history. Belgium offers an impressive array of beer styles, flavors, and breweries ranging from small artisanal businesses to established breweries.

One of the most notable features of Belgian beer culture is the variety of beer styles it offers. Belgium has developed not only the famous Pilsner, but also a plethora of other beer styles, including lambic, dubbel, triple, quadrupel, witbier, gueuze, saison, and many more. Each beer style has its own unique characteristics in terms of aroma, taste, and texture.

Belgian breweries are characterised by their craftsmanship and their pursuit of quality. Many of the best Belgian beers are brewed using traditional methods, often using centuries-old techniques. The Lambic beers, for example, are fermented in open vats with wild yeast strains and bacteria, which gives them their characteristic acidity.

A prominent feature of Belgian beer culture is the use of fruits and spices in some styles of beer. Cherries, peaches, raspberries, and other fruits are often added to create fruity flavors, while spices like cilantro and orange peel add a complex flavor to the beers.

Belgium also has a long tradition of monastic breweries run by monks. These breweries, like the Trappist breweries, produce some of the most sought-after and rare beers in the world. The monks run the breweries not only as economic ventures, but also as part of their monastic life and to support their communities.

Belgian beer culture is also shaped by a rich brewing history that dates back to the Middle Ages. Many breweries have a long family tradition and have been in operation for generations. The beers are often named after the cities or regions where they are brewed and reflect local conditions.

Belgians take their beer seriously and have a long list of customs and rituals around drinking beer. Tasting Belgian beer is a meticulous affair in which the aromas and nuances are appreciated. The right beer glass and the right serving temperature are of great importance in order to enjoy the full taste experience.

In summary, Belgian beer culture is a fascinating part of Belgian identity. The variety of beer styles, the passion of the brewers and the deep-rooted tradition make the world of Belgian beer a unique and rewarding experience for beer lovers around the world. Belgian beer culture is a world of its own to be discovered and appreciated.

Belgian chocolate: the sweet temptation

Known worldwide for its exquisite chocolate creations, Belgium has earned a well-deserved reputation as a chocolate paradise. The Belgian chocolate industry is characterised by centuries-old tradition, craftsmanship and an insatiable passion for high-quality chocolate.

The history of chocolate making in Belgium dates back to the 17th century, when chocolate was first introduced from South America by the Spanish. Belgian chocolatiers soon began perfecting the art of chocolate making, developing unique recipes and techniques.

An outstanding feature of Belgian chocolate is the use of high-quality ingredients. Belgian chocolatiers attach great importance to the selection of first-class cocoa, milk and other raw materials. The quality of the ingredients used is crucial for the taste and texture of the chocolate.

Belgium prides itself on its variety of chocolate varieties and styles. The Belgian chocolate palette ranges from creamy pralines and truffles to crunchy chocolate bars and filled chocolates. Each praline is a small work of art, carefully crafted by hand and often finished with various fillings, including nuts, caramel, fruits and liqueurs.

The Belgian chocolate industry has produced a long list of famous chocolatiers, including brands such as Godiva, Neuhaus, Leonidas, Guylian and many others. These chocolatiers have boutiques and shops all over Belgium and export their chocolate all over the world.

A highlight for chocolate lovers is a visit to a Belgian chocolaterie or chocolate factory. Here, visitors can experience the art of chocolate making up close, from the production of the chocolate mixture to the artisanal production of the chocolates.

Belgian chocolate culture has also given rise to a variety of events and festivals dedicated to chocolate. The Brussels Chocolate Festival, which takes place annually, attracts chocolate lovers from all over the world and offers the opportunity to taste an impressive variety of chocolate products.

Belgian chocolate is not only a delicacy, but also an important economic factor for the country. The chocolate industry creates jobs and contributes to Belgium's economy. Exports of Belgian chocolate are also considerable and help to consolidate the good reputation of Belgian chocolate worldwide.

In summary, Belgian chocolate is a sweet seduction that beguiles the senses and conquers the hearts of chocolate lovers. The combination of tradition, quality and passion has made Belgium one of the best places in the world to enjoy and experience the art of chocolate making. Belgian chocolate is undoubtedly a culinary treasure worth discovering.

Belgian waffles: a culinary delight

Belgian waffles are a world-famous and beloved pastry that has a long tradition in Belgium. These delicious treats are a symbol of Belgian cuisine and are appreciated by both locals and tourists alike.

There are two main types of Belgian waffles: the Brussels waffles and the Liège waffles. Both have their own unique characteristics and are widely used in Belgium.

The Brussels waffles are thin and crispy and have deep grooves that provide the perfect surface to accommodate toppings such as fresh fruit, cream, chocolate sauce or powdered sugar. These waffles are often referred to as "Belgian waffles" abroad and are popular in many parts of the world.

Liège waffles, on the other hand, are thicker and have a soft, chewy texture. They are sweetened and often contain pearl sugar, which caramelizes during baking and gives the waffles a crispy, sweet crust. Liège waffles are a classic street food in Belgium and are often freshly prepared and served warm at markets and festivals.

The preparation of Belgian waffles requires care and precision. The dough is made with ingredients such as flour, eggs, milk, yeast and a pinch of salt. In the case of Liège waffles, the dough is also mixed with pearl sugar. The dough is then baked on a hot waffle iron until golden brown and crispy.

Belgian waffles are not only a popular breakfast and dessert dish, but also an important part of Belgian coffee culture. They are often enjoyed as an accompaniment to a cup of coffee or as an afternoon snack.

Waffle stands and cafes offering Belgian waffles are widespread throughout Belgium. The waffles are often freshly prepared on site and can be personalized according to individual preferences with a variety of toppings.

Belgian waffles are popular not only in Belgium itself, but also internationally and have found a worldwide fan base. The unique textures and flavors of Brussels and Liège waffles have helped them become a culinary symbol of Belgium.

Overall, Belgian waffles are a culinary delight that enriches the food culture of Belgium and is a pleasure for the senses. Whether they're served with fresh berries and cream or with chocolate sauce and ice cream, Belgian waffles are an essential delicacy to try when visiting Belgium.

Belgian cheese: from mild to spicy

Belgium, although not as well-known as some of its European neighbors for its cheese production, has nevertheless developed a rich and diverse cheese tradition. From mild, creamy varieties to spicy, aged variations, Belgium offers a wide range of cheeses that delight the palates of cheese lovers around the world.

One of the most famous Belgian cheeses is the "Herve" or "Limburger". This type of cheese comes from the Liège region and is known for its intense smell and strong taste. Herve cheese is made from cow's milk and matures in special conditions that develop its characteristic rind and taste.

Another popular Belgian cheese is the "Passendale", which is produced near Ypres. This semi-hard cheese is characterized by its mild, slightly nutty flavor and is often eaten in sandwiches or as a snack.

The "Bouquet des Moines" is a semi-hard cheese made by the monks of Chimay. This cheese has a soft, creamy texture and a mild, slightly sour taste.

The "Crottin de Chavignol" is a small, round goat's cheese variant from Belgium, produced near Namur. This cheese has a dry, crumbly texture and a fresh, slightly sour taste.

Belgium is also known for its cheeses with fruits and spices. The "Herve au Miel" is a Herve cheese that is refined with honey and has a sweet, spicy note. The "Maredsous" is a semi-hard cheese with herbs and spices produced near the abbey of the same name.

Belgian cheese production has seen a boom in recent years as more and more small farms develop and launch innovative cheeses. These artisanal cheeses offer a wide range of flavors and textures that reflect the diversity of Belgian cheese culture.

Belgium is also proud of its cheese affinity, the art of maturing cheese. In affinage companies, cheeses are matured in special storage rooms under controlled conditions to develop their taste and texture. Belgium has a growing number of affineurs who help promote the quality and diversity of the Belgian cheese scene.

In conclusion, Belgian cheese offers a wide range of aromas and flavors, from mild to spicy. The Belgian cheese tradition, whether old or new, is characterized by quality and craftsmanship and offers an exciting opportunity to discover the culinary diversity of Belgium.

The Belgian language: Dutch, French and German

Belgium, a country of only about 11 million inhabitants, is a remarkably multilingual country. This linguistic richness reflects the country's complex history and diverse regions. Three main languages are spoken in Belgium: Dutch, French and German.

Dutch is the most widely spoken language in Belgium and is spoken by the majority of the population in Flanders, the northern part of the country. This variant of Dutch is often referred to as "Flemish". It is the official language in Flanders and is used in schools, media and the government. Flemish culture and identity are closely linked to the Dutch language, and there are some regional differences in pronunciation and vocabulary within Flanders.

French is mainly spoken in Wallonia, in the south of Belgium, and is the official language of this region. In Brussels, the capital of Belgium, French is also an official language and is spoken by a significant part of the population. French culture and influences are strongly present in Wallonia and Brussels, and the French language plays an important role in education, media and government.

The German-speaking community of Belgium is a small but significant minority in the east of the country, in the region of East Belgium. German is the official language here and is used in educational institutions and administration. The German language and culture are alive in this community, and it cultivates its own cultural traditions and identities.

It is important to emphasize that Belgium has a complex political structure due to its linguistic diversity. The country is federally organised and consists of three regions with their own governments: Flanders, Wallonia and the Brussels-Capital Region. These regions are linguistically defined, with the Brussels-Capital Region being bilingual.

Belgium's linguistic diversity is a reflection of the country's cultural riches and reflects the history and diversity of its inhabitants. Despite the challenges that come with this diversity, Belgium is a remarkable example of the peaceful coexistence of people from different linguistic and cultural backgrounds. This makes Belgium a unique and fascinating country to explore and understand.

The cultural diversity of Belgium

Belgium, a small country in the heart of Europe, stands out for its extraordinary cultural diversity. This diversity is the result of a rich history, geographical location and complex political structure. Belgium is a country where different cultures, languages and traditions are interwoven in a very small space.

One of the most striking cultural differences in Belgium is the language. As mentioned in a previous chapter, three main languages are spoken in Belgium: Dutch, French and German. This linguistic diversity reflects the country's history and regional differences. Dutch dominates in Flanders, French in Wallonia and German in the East Belgium region. The bilingual Brussels-Capital Region is a melting pot of cultures, where both French and Dutch are official.

However, Belgium's cultural diversity is not only evident in its languages, but also in the country's art, architecture and gastronomy. Belgium has a rich tradition in the visual arts, from famous painters such as René Magritte and Pieter Bruegel the Elder to contemporary artists. Belgium's architecture ranges from medieval castles to Gothic cathedrals to modern buildings in Brussels and Antwerp.

Belgian cuisine is famous for its variety and quality. Belgian chocolate, waffles, beers and cheeses are internationally known and appreciated by gourmets. Belgian gastronomy is characterised by regional influences, with each region having its own culinary specialities.

Belgian culture is also marked by festivals and events, including the famous Binche Carnival, the Genk Flower Festival and the Ostend Film Festival. Belgium has a vibrant music scene that ranges from classical to pop to electronic music.

Belgium's cultural diversity is also reflected in its political structure. The country is organised on a federal basis and consists of three regions (Flanders, Wallonia and the Brussels-Capital Region) and the three language communities (Flemish, French and German). This federal structure allows regions and communities to maintain their own cultural identity and autonomy.

In conclusion, Belgium's cultural diversity is one of its most distinctive features. This small country in the heart of Europe is a melting pot of different cultures, languages and traditions. The coexistence and interaction of this diversity makes Belgium a fascinating and unique place worth exploring and understanding.

Belgian festivals and customs

Belgium is a country rich in traditional festivals and customs that are deeply rooted in its history and culture. These celebrations and rituals reflect the cultural diversity and regional differences of the country.

One of the most famous festivals in Belgium is the Binche Carnival, which is recognized as a UNESCO World Heritage Site. This carnival, which takes place in the Walloon town of Binche, has a long tradition and attracts thousands of visitors every year. The highlight of the Binche Carnival is the "Gilles", a group of masked people who wear colourful costumes, wooden shoes and feathered hats. The Gilles throw oranges into the crowd and dance through the streets, accompanied by traditional music. This carnival is a unique spectacle that reflects the cheerfulness and sense of community of Belgian culture.

Another notable festival in Belgium is the Ommegang Festival in Brussels, which commemorates the arrival of Emperor Charles V in 1549. This historic event is celebrated with a magnificent parade, where costumed performers re-enact history and depict historical figures. The Ommegang Festival is an opportunity for Brussels residents and visitors to immerse themselves in the city's rich history. In Flanders, the "Doudou" of Mons is a traditional festival that takes place every year in June. This is a religious procession in which a large golden carriage with a statue of the Virgin Mary is pulled through the streets of Mons. This festival, which dates back to the 14th century, attracts many believers and onlookers and is an important event in Walloon culture.

The Belgian Christmas season is marked by numerous traditions. Christmas markets are held in many towns and villages, where handmade gifts, Christmas treats and mulled wine are offered. Belgium is also known for its Christmas lights and festively decorated cities that create a warm and welcoming atmosphere.

Another special tradition in Belgium is the "Sinterklaas", which is similar to St. Nicholas' Day. On 6 December, Sinterklaas, accompanied by his helpers, the "Zwarte Pieten", brings gifts to the children. This custom is widespread in Belgium and the Netherlands and has a long history.

Belgium is also famous for its culinary customs, such as Easter dinner with chocolate bunnies and enjoying Belgian beer on various occasions.

In conclusion, Belgium offers a rich variety of festivals and customs that reflect the cultural and regional diversity of the country. These traditions and celebrations are an important part of Belgian identity and help keep the country's history and culture alive.

The Belgian fashion industry

Belgium may be a small country, but it has a huge influence in the fashion industry. The Belgian fashion industry has built a reputation for creativity, innovation and quality around the world. This chapter is dedicated to the fascinating world of Belgian fashion.

One of the most famous names in Belgian fashion is undoubtedly Raf Simons. Born in Neerpelt, Belgium, the designer has made his mark on the fashion industry with his minimalist and avant-garde designs. Simons has been celebrated for his work at prestigious fashion houses such as Jil Sander and Dior and has received several awards for his collections.

Another outstanding Belgian designer is Dries Van Noten. His label, founded in Antwerp in 1986, stands for timeless elegance and refined details. Van Noten has earned an international reputation for its exquisite fabrics and pattern work, and its collections are appreciated worldwide.

The "Antwerp Six" are a group of Belgian designers who gained international recognition in the 1980s. In addition to Dries Van Noten, this group also includes Ann Demeulemeester, Dirk Bikkembergs, Walter Van Beirendonck, Marina

Yee and Dirk Van Saene. Together, they have brought Belgian fashion to the world stage, shaping a distinctive style that is characterized by subversive elements and creative freedom.

Antwerp, the largest city in Flanders, has become an important centre for Belgian fashion. The city is home to the prestigious Royal Academy of Fine Arts, whose graduates are often among the industry's up-and-coming talents. Antwerp also hosts Antwerp Fashion Week, an annual event where Belgian designers showcase their latest collections.

Belgian fashion is known for its versatility. It ranges from avant-garde haute couture to casual street fashion. Belgian designers have a keen sense of experimentation and innovation, which makes their collections exciting and unique time and time again.

It is worth noting that Belgium is also appreciated for its high-quality fabrics and tailoring. The Belgian fashion industry places a high value on craftsmanship and quality, which is reflected in the durability and sophistication of its products.

In conclusion, the Belgian fashion industry offers an impressive variety of talents and styles. From the innovative designs of Raf Simons to the timeless elegance of Dries Van Noten, Belgium has taken a firm place in the fashion industry, helping to showcase the country's creative diversity. Belgian fashion is an important part of the global fashion world and will continue to shine with its unique flair and excellence.

Arts and crafts in Belgium

Belgium is not only known for its fashion industry and chocolate, but also for its rich heritage of handicrafts and craftsmanship. These traditions go far back into the country's history and are an important part of Belgian culture.

One of the most famous forms of handicrafts in Belgium is lace making. Belgian lace, especially the so-called "Bruges lace", is known worldwide for its delicacy and quality. This craftsmanship has a long history and has been passed down through generations by skilled craftsmen. Bruges, a city often referred to as the "Venice of the North," is a center for lace-making and offers visitors the chance to experience this traditional craft firsthand.

Another important handicraft in Belgium is pottery. The city of Durbuy in Wallonia is famous for its ceramic production and has a long tradition of producing ceramics. These handmade products are appreciated for their quality and beauty.

Carpet making is another example of Belgian craftsmanship. The city of Tournai in Wallonia is known for its carpets, especially the "Tapis de Tournai". These hand-knotted rugs are characterized by their artistic patterns and high quality.

Belgian craftsmanship also extends to the production of woodwork. The city of Malmedy in the Ardennes is famous for its wood carvings and woodwork. Traditional products such as wooden cuckoo clocks and hand-carved furniture are made here.

There is also a long tradition of glassmaking in Belgium. The town of La Louvière in Wallonia is known for its glassblowing art, where elaborate glassware and vases are made.

Belgian craftsmanship is characterised by attention to detail, care and a strong sense of tradition. These handmade products are not only appreciated in Belgium, but are also highly valued internationally.

To sum up, handicrafts and handicrafts occupy an important place in Belgian culture. The traditions and skills that have been passed down through generations reflect the creative diversity and cultural heritage of the country. Belgium is proud of its craftsmanship and will continue to cultivate and preserve these precious traditions.

Belgian folklore and folk music

Belgian folklore and folk music are deeply rooted in the country's culture and reflect the diversity of Belgium's regions. Belgium, with its different communities and languages, has a rich tradition of folklore and folk music, which is passed down from generation to generation.

One of the most famous forms of Belgian folk music is the song "La Brabançonne". This song is the official national anthem of Belgium and has a long history. It was first sung in the 19th century during the Belgian independence movement and eventually became the country's anthem.

Flanders, the Dutch-speaking region of Belgium, has a rich tradition of folk music, often accompanied by bagpipes, violins, and accordions. This music is often performed at festivals and celebrations and reflects the rural culture and way of life.

Wallonia, the French-speaking region of Belgium, also has a vibrant folk music tradition. Here, accordions, guitars and flutes are often used to accompany traditional songs. Wallonia's folk music is often inspired by stories and legends and is performed on various occasions, from weddings to village festivals.

In the Ardennes, a mountain range in Belgium, folk music is characterized by the rustic way of life and natural elements. Here you can often hear the melodies of ship's horns, violins and flutes, which reflect the beauty of nature and the history of the region.

Belgian folklore also extends to traditional festivals and customs. An example of this is the famous parade of "Gilles" in Binche, which is a UNESCO World Heritage Site. This parade takes place during the carnival and the participants wear colorful costumes and masked faces. It is a spectacular event that celebrates Belgian tradition and creativity.

Overall, Belgian folklore and folk music shows the country's cultural diversity and pride in its cultural roots. These traditions are carefully maintained and are an important part of Belgium's heritage. They offer insights into the different regions and communities of the country and contribute to Belgium's cultural identity.

The Belgian Film Industry

The Belgian film industry has made a remarkable contribution to the international film world over the years. Belgium may be a small country, but it has a vibrant and diverse film scene that has gained recognition both nationally and internationally.

The beginnings of Belgian film date back to the late 19th century, when the Lumière brothers screened their groundbreaking films in Belgium. However, these early attempts at film production were short-lived at first, and it took a few decades for a stable film industry to develop.

During the 20th century, Belgium began to develop its own cinematic identity. A milestone in the history of Belgian film was the creation of the Centre du Cinéma in the 1960s, which enabled the promotion and financing of Belgian film projects. This led to the emergence of a new generation of talented filmmakers, including the Dardenne brothers, who are internationally known for their socially engaged films.

The Belgian film industry has earned a reputation for diversity and innovation due to its cultural diversity and its promotion of creative freedom. Films such as "The Child" and "Rosetta" by the Dardenne brothers and "The White Ribbon" by Michael Haneke have won awards at international film festivals and have made Belgian cinema famous worldwide.

In addition to recognition at international film festivals, Belgium has also developed its own national film industry, which produces films in the three national languages of Dutch, French and German. Belgian film production ranges from artistic dramas and comedies to documentaries and animations.

Another important aspect of the Belgian film industry is the promotion of young talent and cooperation with international partners. Belgian film schools and institutions have produced talented filmmakers who are able to produce innovative and engaging films.

The Belgian film industry is also known for its festivals such as the Flanders-Ghent International Film Festival and the Brussels International Film Festival, which help to increase the visibility and influence of Belgian cinema.

In conclusion, the Belgian film industry has a rich and diverse history, marked by talent, innovation and cultural diversity. Despite its modest size, Belgium has occupied a significant place in the international film world and will continue to produce films that deserve the attention and recognition of a worldwide audience.

Sports and leisure in Belgium

Belgium offers a wide range of sports and leisure opportunities for locals and visitors alike. Belgium's enthusiasm for sport is reflected in their active participation in various activities.

One of the most popular sports in Belgium is football. The country has a long tradition in football and is proud of its national teams, which participate in international tournaments such as the FIFA World Cup and the UEFA European Championship. The Belgian Pro League is the highest football league in the country, and matches regularly attract large crowds.

Cycling is another very popular leisure activity in Belgium. The country has a well-developed network of cycle paths and offers a picturesque backdrop for cyclists. Cycling is so popular that Belgium has produced some of the best cyclists in the world, including Eddy Merckx, who is considered one of the greatest cyclists of all time.

Tennis, hockey, volleyball and basketball are other popular sports in Belgium. The country also has an active motorsport scene and is home to the famous Circuit de Spa-Francorchamps, one of the most challenging circuits in the world, which regularly hosts Formula 1 races and other motorsport events.

For nature lovers, the Ardennes in Belgium offers a wealth of outdoor activities such as hiking, climbing, canoeing and white water rafting. The region is a popular destination for adventure seekers who want to explore the stunning scenery and diverse wildlife.

Belgium is also known for its tradition of cycling, especially for hosting cycling races such as the Tour of Flanders and Liège-Bastogne-Liège, which are among the most important classics in cycling.

There are a variety of leisure options in the cities, including museums, theaters, concerts, and restaurants. Belgium is also known for its beer culture, and tasting Belgian beer is a popular leisure activity for locals and tourists alike.

Belgium's love of sport and leisure is reflected in the variety of activities on offer and people's passion for physical activity and entertainment. Whether you're interested in traditional sports, outdoor adventures, or cultural experiences, Belgium has something for everyone.

Belgian hospitality and etiquette

Belgian hospitality is characterised by a warm and friendly attitude towards guests. Belgians are proud to welcome their visitors and give them a pleasant time in their country.

An important tradition in Belgium is hospitality when eating. Belgian meals are often social events where family and friends come together to enjoy good food and company. If you are invited to a Belgian house, it is customary to bring a guest gift, such as a bottle of wine or chocolate, to express your appreciation.

When entering a Belgian home, it is customary to take off your shoes, especially if the host suggests it. This is seen as a sign of respect. In restaurants, it is customary to tip, usually about 10% of the bill amount.

In Belgium, it is important to be polite and respectful. Greeting with a firm handshake is common, and it's polite to maintain eye contact when talking to someone. When accepting an invitation, it's wise to be on time to show your appreciation for the hosts.

Belgian etiquette also emphasizes table manners. It is customary to put your hands on the table, but your elbows should not be rested on the table.

You are expected to place your cutlery neatly on the plate when you have finished eating to signal that you have emptied your plate.

In terms of communication, it is important to be respectful and express yourself in an appropriate tone. Belgians are usually polite and respectful of others, and you are expected to do the same.

In terms of clothing, Belgium is rather conservative, especially in business environments. You are expected to dress appropriately and look clean and well-groomed.

In summary, Belgian hospitality is characterized by warmth and respect. Adherence to the country's etiquette and cultural norms is appreciated and helps to build positive relationships with the locals and make your time in Belgium enjoyable.

Belgian souvenirs and souvenirs

When you visit Belgium, you'll have the opportunity to pick up a variety of unique souvenirs and souvenirs that will not only serve as mementos of your trip, but also make gifts for friends and family. Belgium is known for its high-quality products and handmade items that make great souvenirs.

1. Belgian chocolate: Belgium is known worldwide for its exquisite chocolate creations. When visiting the country, be sure to pick up some of the best Belgian chocolates and chocolate bars. They will be available in a variety of shops and chocolatiers, including famous brands such as Neuhaus, Godiva and Leonidas.
2. Belgian beer: Belgium is famous for its diverse and high-quality range of beers. You can buy different types of Belgian beer in bottles or cans to take home. Some varieties are seasonally and regionally limited, which makes them special souvenirs.
3. Top products: Belgian lace is a traditional craft and a sought-after souvenir. You can find handmade lace products such as tablecloths, napkins and lace accessories in many shops and markets.

4. Diamonds: Antwerp, the diamond city of Belgium, offers an abundance of diamonds and jewellery. If you are looking for an exclusive souvenir, a piece of Belgian diamond jewellery is an excellent choice.
5. Comics: Belgium has a rich tradition in the field of comics, and you can find Belgian comics and merchandising items in specialized comic shops. Famous characters such as Tintin come from Belgium.
6. Ceramics and porcelain: Belgian ceramic and porcelain products are known for their quality and attractive design. Pottery, tableware and decorative pieces are available as souvenirs.
7. Waffles: Belgian waffles are world-famous, and you can take them home in the form of waffle mixes or special waffle tools to experience the taste of Belgium in your own kitchen.
8. Fashion and accessories: Belgium has an up-and-coming fashion industry, and you can pick up fashionable clothes, shoes, and accessories from Belgian designers that serve as stylish souvenirs.
9. Handicrafts: Belgian artisans make a variety of handmade products, including woodwork, glassware, and textiles. These products are often unique and can serve as special souvenirs.

When buying souvenirs in Belgium, it is advisable to visit local markets and shops to discover a wide range of authentic products. Keep in mind that when you buy goods in Belgium, you may be able to claim VAT back if you are a non-EU citizen, and that some items will need to be declared when leaving the country. Belgian souvenirs are not only memories of your trip, but also a way to take home the country's rich culture and traditions.

The best tourist attractions in Belgium

Belgium offers a wealth of impressive sights and attractions for visitors from all over the world. From historic cities to stunning landscapes, here are some of the best tourist attractions to explore in Belgium:

1. **The historic center of Bruges**: Bruges, often referred to as the "Venice of the North," is known for its well-preserved medieval buildings, canals, and charming alleyways. The historic center of Bruges is a UNESCO World Heritage Site and a real treasure for lovers of architecture and history.
2. **The Grand-Place in Brussels**: The central market square of Brussels, the Grand-Place, is a masterpiece of architecture and a UNESCO World Heritage Site. The magnificent buildings, including the City Hall and the Maison du Roi, are impressive examples of the Baroque architectural style.
3. **The Atomium**: This futuristic building in Brussels represents an enlarged iron molecule and is a symbol of the belief in scientific progress. Visitors can climb into the spheres of the Atomium and enjoy impressive views of the city.

4. **Antwerp Cathedral**: The Cathedral of Our Lady in Antwerp is one of the most impressive Gothic buildings in Europe. Its 123-meter-high tower dominates the city and houses masterpieces by famous painters such as Peter Paul Rubens.
5. **Gravensteen Castle in Ghent**: This medieval castle in the heart of Ghent is an impressive example of a well-preserved fortress. Visitors can explore the interior and learn more about the history of this impressive structure.
6. **The Waterloo Battlefield**: This historic site, located south of Brussels, was the site of the famous Battle of Waterloo in 1815, in which Napoleon was defeated. The visitor center and memorial offer insight into this crucial historical episode.
7. **The Ardennes**: This wooded region in the south of Belgium offers an impressive natural backdrop with picturesque rivers, hiking trails and outdoor activities. The Ardennes are a popular destination for nature lovers and adventurers.
8. **The Mini-Europe in Brussels**: In this miniature park, visitors can admire miniature models of famous European landmarks. It's a fun way to explore the diversity of European heritage in one place.
9. **The Hôtel de Ville in Liège**: The Town Hall of Liège is a magnificent

Renaissance-style building and a symbol of the city. The ornate decorations and architecture make it an impressive sight to behold.
10. **The canals of Mechelen**: Mechelen, a charming city in the Flanders region, has beautiful canals that allow for a peaceful stroll or boat ride. The picturesque surroundings and the historic buildings along the canals are worth seeing.

These are just a few of the highlights that Belgium has to offer visitors. The country is rich in cultural treasures, breathtaking nature and fascinating history to discover. Whatever your interests, there is always something in Belgium that will excite you.

Secret Treasures: Hidden Gems in Belgium

While Belgium is known for its well-known landmarks and tourist attractions, the country also holds a wealth of hidden gems that are often overlooked by visitors. These lesser-known places offer unique insights into the culture, history and natural beauty of Belgium. Here are some of these secret gems:

1. **The Caves of Han**: The Ardennes are home to the impressive Caves of Han, an underground cave system that is often overlooked. Visitors can take a magical journey through these natural wonders and admire the stalactites and stalagmites.
2. **The Abbey of Villers-la-Ville**: Located near Brussels, this well-preserved 12th-century Cistercian abbey is a tranquil retreat. The ruins and gardens of the abbey provide a picturesque backdrop for walks and photography.
3. **The Belfry of Mons**: Mons, a charming town in Wallonia, is home to an impressive belfry that is a UNESCO World Heritage Site. The tower not only offers a great view, but also a rich history.
4. **The sunflower fields of Flanders**: In summer, the sunflower fields in the Flemish region bloom and offer a

colourful spectacle. This natural spectacle is often overlooked, but it is a true feast for the senses.
5. **The Blegny Mine**: This disused coal mine near Liège gives visitors an insight into the hard work of the miners. The guided tour of the mine is instructive and impressive.
6. **The Château de Seneffe**: This elegant castle near Brussels is home to a remarkable silver museum and surrounds itself with magnificent gardens and ponds. It is a place of peace and beauty.
7. **The Durbuy**: Described as the smallest city in the world, Durbuy is a picturesque village in the Ardennes. The narrow streets and medieval buildings give it an enchanting charm.
8. **The Domaine Solvay**: This private estate near Brussels is home to a magnificent park and castle. The gardens are a perfect place for a relaxing stroll.
9. **Tournai Cathedral**: While Tournai Cathedral is less well-known than its counterparts in other cities, it is a remarkable example of Romanesque architecture and is home to impressive works of art.
10. **The Hoge Kempen National Park**: This national park in Flanders is a paradise for nature lovers and hikers. It offers a rich

variety of flora and fauna as well as well-marked hiking trails.

These secret treasures of Belgium are waiting to be discovered by curious travellers. They add an extra dimension to the country and allow you to experience its diversity and beauty in all its facets.

Closing remarks

In this book, we have taken a fascinating journey through the country of Belgium and explored its diverse history, culture, nature and way of life. Belgium, a small country in Western Europe, has a rich and complex past that dates back to the Romans. Over the centuries, it has experienced various dominations, from the Romans to the Franks, the Burgundians, the Habsburgs and the Spaniards. The Belgian Revolution of 1830 led to the creation of modern Belgium, which remains a constitutional monarchy to this day.

The diversity of Belgian culture is reflected in the different regions of the country, where Dutch, French and German languages are spoken. Belgium prides itself on its culinary delights, from chocolate to beer to waffles and cheese. Belgian architecture and art have produced impressive masterpieces over the centuries, including Gothic cathedrals, Baroque castles, and surrealist paintings.

Belgian literature, music and the film industry have also found their place on the world stage, and Belgian authors, musicians and filmmakers have gained international recognition. The country also has a rich tradition in the field of comics, with famous characters such as Tintin.

The nature of Belgium is shaped by the Ardennes, a beautiful natural paradise with dense forests, rivers and picturesque villages. The flora and fauna of the country are diverse and provide habitat for a wide range of animal and plant species.

In the European Union, Belgium plays an important role as the seat of many EU institutions, especially in Brussels. Belgian politics and constitution are characterised by federal structures that grant autonomy to the different regions of the country.

Belgium also has a rich tradition of festivals and customs that are celebrated throughout the year. From carnival parades to Easter markets to Christmas markets, there's always a reason to celebrate.

Belgian hospitality and etiquette are an important part of daily life, and Belgians are known for their warmth and friendliness towards visitors.

Finally, in this book, we've also explored some of Belgium's best tourist attractions, from the historic cities of Brussels, Antwerp, Ghent, and Bruges to the natural wonders of the Ardennes and the country's hidden gems.

Belgium is undoubtedly a country worth exploring, and I hope this book has helped you appreciate the beauty and diversity of this fascinating country. There is still much to discover and experience, and I encourage you to take your own journey through Belgium and reveal the secrets and treasures this country has to offer. Have fun discovering Belgium!

Made in the USA
Middletown, DE
31 October 2024